BALLERINAS OF SADLER'S WELLS

DANCERS OF TO-DAY NO. 5

MARGOT FONTEYN IN GISELLE, ACT I

BALLERINAS

OF
SADLER'S WELLS

by

HUGH FISHER

LONDON
ADAM AND CHARLES BLACK

FIRST PUBLISHED 1954
REPRINTED WITH CORRECTIONS AND
SOME NEW ILLUSTRATIONS 1956

A. & C. BLACK LTD.
4, 5 & 6 SOHO SQUARE
LONDON, W.I

CONTENTS

MADE IN GREAT BRITAIN
PRINTED BY MORRISON AND GIBB LIMITED, LONDON AND EDINBURGH

INTRODUCTION

In the four or five great ballet companies of the world which are State or semi-State institutions, the term ballerina is used officially by only two of them, although with the exception of Sadler's Wells they all define with great exactitude the ranks through which a dancer may progress. At the Paris Opéra, there is a highly codified system of progression, and annual examinations for promotion are held. The highest rank is *première danseuse*, the equivalent of ballerina, with sometimes exceptional elevation to *première danseuse étoile*, the equivalent of prima ballerina. In Denmark, in the Royal Danish Ballet, which has produced so many fine dancers in recent years, the status of a dancer may progress almost like a career in the Civil Service but the term ballerina is rarely used. In Russia, in Imperialist days, as recalled in Tamara Karsavina's *Theatre Street*, and under the present régime, there is a system of promotion, similar to the Paris Opéra's, to the rank of ballerina and special honour may be given to an outstanding dancer such as Ulanova.

The Sadler's Wells Ballet, which is partly subsidised by the State through the Arts Council, is relatively free from any control in the management of its affairs, and it has avoided the rigid systems which have grown up elsewhere. It has retained a flexibility in its organisation and in its advancement of dancers, which ensure that merit in performance is the only criterion for promotion. The progress of its dancers has always been by a process of trial and error: dancers have been given opportunities to dance leading rôles, and if they have been successful, prepared carefully for other leading parts, until in time they have become principal dancers of the Company and acknowledged as ballerinas. Recently, official announcements have been made when a dancer has been deemed worthy to be described as a ballerina, but the process of trial and error continues, and long may it do so.

Ballerinas cannot be produced at regular intervals, and there are only a few dancers in a generation who are likely to achieve this status, but, as this little book seeks to show, the Sadler's Wells Ballet has been most fortunate. Several of its ballerinas have been students at the Sadler's Wells School, and most of them have danced in the *corps de ballet* before becoming soloists. Years of hard work, allied to the talents that nature has bestowed upon them, have earned them their title. Ninette de Valois, Alicia Markova, Pearl Argyle, Margot Fonteyn, Mary Honer, Pamela May, Beryl Grey, Moira Shearer, Violetta Elvin, Nadia Nerina, Rowena Jackson and Svetlana Beriosova, the most recent to be promoted ballerina: it is a magnificent list for a company which has been in existence for barely twenty-five years.

NINETTE DE VALOIS

An announcement in *The Dancing Times* towards the end of 1930 gave details of a new ballet company to be formed by Miss Lilian Baylis of the Old Vic. " For some years past," the announcement read, " Miss Lilian Baylis has cherished an ambition to establish for the first time in theatrical history a permanent ballet in a repertory theatre. The Sadler's Wells Ballet Company will have at the beginning six or seven salaried dancers with Ninette de Valois as prima ballerina, director and principal choreographist."

Anthony

SWANILDA IN COPPÉLIA

Even if Miss Baylis used the term " prima ballerina " somewhat extravagantly to describe the leading dancer of a small troupe of dancers, it should be remembered that in 1930 Miss de Valois was one of the best known English dancers of the day. She had danced with Anton Dolin in revue and in music-hall programmes, and she had been *première danseuse* at the Royal Opera House, Covent Garden, during the opera season. She had danced in London with Massine's and Lopokova's Companies in the early twenties, and, most important of all, she had been a soloist in Diaghilev's Company for the best part of two years, appearing in some thirty ballets including : ten of Fokine's ballets, eight of Massine's, a two-act version of *Le Lac des Cygnes*, and *Aurora's Wedding*, and eight new ballets including Nijinska's *Les Biches*, *Le Train Bleu*, and *Les Noces*, Balanchine's *Le Chant de Rossignol* and Massine's *Zephyr et Flore*. When she joined Diaghilev she was already an accomplished dancer, and the months of hard, intensive work with Diaghilev's Company improved her already fine technique. She earned Diaghilev's special praise for the " finger variation " in *Aurora's Wedding*, and if she had not left the Company of her own accord, it is likely that she would have been given many more important solo rôles.

In the first few seasons of the Vic-Wells Ballet she danced leading parts in most of the new ballets created for the Company, revealing in such ballets as *Regatta* and *Douanes* a delightful sense of comedy and fun. In *Coppélia* she was a gay and vivacious Swanilda. On one historic occasion she danced the *pas de trois* from *Le Lac des Cygnes*, with Markova and Dolin.

As the Company grew she devoted more of her time to administration, direction and teaching, and she made her last appearance as a dancer in 1936, as the maid, Webster, in Ashton's *A Wedding Bouquet*. She danced this part again at the 21st Birthday of the Company, held at Sadler's Wells Theatre in 1951.

IN BARABAU

Anthony

ALICIA MARKOVA

Alicia Markova was the bright star of the early years of the Vic-Wells Ballet. The Company owes her an immense debt : she attracted a large public to Sadler's Wells, who came to see *her* dance rather than to see the young dancers of the Vic-Wells Ballet, although many of them became constant supporters of the Company.

With Markova in the Company, Ninette de Valois was able to embark on the production of the great classical ballets : *Le Lac des Cygnes*, Act II, was presented, followed later by the complete ballet with Markova as Odette-Odile ; *Giselle* was produced, followed shortly afterwards by *Casse-Noisette*.

Anthony

IN LES RENDEZVOUS

If the Company was grateful to Markova, for her part she was equally grateful for the opportunity given to her to dance regularly in ballet, and more particularly in classical ballet, as opposed to the commercial engagements in revues and in cinemas, which were then the only alternatives by which a dancer could earn her living. Thus her period with the Vic-Wells Ballet was of immense importance to her development as a dancer.

Since Diaghilev's death in 1929, and the dispersal of his Company of which she was a most promising member, she had had little opportunity of dancing until Marie Rambert started the Ballet Club, towards the end of 1930, and the formation of the Camargo Society the same year. In the Ballet Club on Sunday evenings she danced in the miniature ballets created by Ashton, Antony Tudor and others, and in *Le Carnaval* and several classical *pas de deux*, but the Ballet Club, with its limited resources, could neither employ her permanently nor provide her with the rôles that a dancer must dance if she is to develop into a ballerina. The Vic-Wells Ballet gave her these opportunities.

Markova first appeared with the Vic-Wells Ballet on 30th January 1932, and, as a guest artist, she danced frequently with the Company until her engagement as a permanent member for the Autumn Season of 1933. She stayed with the Company until 1st June 1935. She returned to dance with the Sadler's Wells Ballet thirteen years later, at Covent Garden. During that time the Company had become one of the great ballet companies of the world, and Markova, its one-time prima ballerina, had become the best-known dancer in the world to-day.

IN LES SYLPHIDES

9

IN THE LORD OF BURLEIGH

Anthony

PEARL ARGYLE

When Alicia Markova left the Vic-Wells Company in 1935, to form her own company with Anton Dolin, no famous dancer was engaged to take her place. Miss de Valois believed that the Company was almost strong enough to stand on its own, but to strengthen the limited number of leading dancers she engaged Pearl Argyle.

She was an accomplished dancer of exceptional beauty, who had danced with the Ballet Club since its earliest days, creating leading rôles in many of its new ballets. She has been described " as an exquisite artist in miniature," and she did not succeed entirely in projecting her personality in a theatre many times the size of the tiny Mercury Theatre.

One of her most successful parts in the Vic-Wells Company was as the Fairy in Ashton's *Baiser de la Fée*—in this she had

a new-found authority, and the beauty of her line and her assured technique were seen to advantage. Among the other ballets in which she danced, she was outstanding in *Pomona, The Gods Go A-Begging, Le Roi Nu, The Lord of Burleigh, Les Sylphides, Le Carnaval,* and in the Aurora *pas de deux.*

She started dancing too late in life to acquire a sufficiently strong technique for the great classical ballets, but within her limits she was a great artist, with a warmth and charm of personality that endeared her to dancers and audience alike. She had an admirable sense of the theatre, and in rôles that suited her she has had no equal : the Goddess turned Serving Maid in *The Gods Go A-Begging* and the Empress in *Le Roi Nu* are two rôles with which her name will be always remembered.

PEARL ARGYLE AND ROBERT HELPMANN

AURORA

MARGOT FONTEYN

Margot Fonteyn is the first ballerina to be produced by Sadler's Wells, and from the time she appeared as an anonymous snowflake in *Casse-Noisette* in 1934 until to-day, all her life has been spent with the Company, apart from a few special visits she has paid as guest ballerina to other companies, and for a short season with Roland Petit's Company in Paris.

When Markova left the Company in 1935, Fonteyn succeeded to some of her rôles, and in time the great classical ballets were revived for her. Immature as her performances were, her first Odette in December 1935 and her first Giselle in 1937, revealed beyond doubt that here was a dancer who

Anthony

IN LES RENDEZVOUS

IN HOMAGE TO THE QUEEN

Houston Rogers

would one day become a prima ballerina. Since then she has burnished until they shine with perfection — Odette-Odile, Giselle and Aurora, and her parts in the modern repertoire: Sylvia, Cinderella, Chloé, the Firebird and others.

Her dancing is so much more than technical virtuosity—one is not conscious of her dancing but only of the effect she creates. As with a great actor, so it is with Fonteyn: she is the character she dances. Her emotional range, her dramatic powers, her musicality, her ability to project feeling, and the magnificence of her dancing—all are there, combined and integrated into a performance of breathtaking beauty. The great artist never rests content, and Fonteyn, *prima ballerina assoluta* of the Sadler's Wells Ballet, is no exception.

Her pre-eminence as a dancer was recognised in the New Year's Honours for 1956, when she became Dame Margot Fonteyn, D.B.E., the first dancer to be so honoured by the Sovereign while still dancing.

Felix Fonteyn

WITH MICHAEL SOMES IN SYLVIA

MARY HONER

When Mary Honer joined the Vic-Wells Ballet in 1935 she was already an experienced dancer with a virtuoso technique. She had studied under first-class teachers including Margaret Craske, Legat and Preobrajenska, but hitherto she had danced only in revue and musical comedy, and it took her a little time to shed the mannerisms that are part of a musical comedy dancer's stock-in-trade. She excelled in those parts which permitted her to display her magnificent virtuosity. In *Les Patineurs* her *fouettés* had an ease and brilliance that never failed to astonish and delight the audience, and her Sugar Plum Fairy in *Casse-Noisette* was another rôle well suited to her virtuosity. Her acting and mime improved greatly after she had been with the Company for some time : she was an incredibly silly Bride in *A Wedding Bouquet*, and most moving as the Betrayed Girl in *The Rake's Progress*. In

Anthony

SWANILDA IN COPPÉLIA

The Sleeping Princess, she was magnificent in the Bluebird *pas de deux*, and on one occasion when Pamela May injured herself at a performance of *The Sleeping Princess*, she stepped in without hesitation and danced the Lilac Fairy as well as her own part, with an ease and authority that never betrayed the slightest nervousness. She danced leading rôles in most of the Company's repertoire, from Columbine in *Le Carnaval* and the Waltz in *Les Sylphides* to the Foolish Virgin in *The Wise and Foolish Virgins*. She came too late to classical ballet to develop fully the range of emotion, the sense of line and the musicality that these rôles demand, and her Odette-Odile was not outstanding. But in *Coppélia* she was completely successful. Her gaiety and her sense of fun made her an ideal Swanilda, and she was sadly missed in this rôle when she left the Company during the war years.

Anthony

IN THE BLUEBIRD PAS DE DEUX

Anthony

IN LE LAC DES CYGNES

Felix Fonteyn

THE PRINCESS-MOTHER IN LE LAC DES CYGNES

PAMELA MAY

To-day we see Pamela May as a guest artist: as the Queen in *The Sleeping Beauty*, and the Princess-Mother in *Le Lac des Cygnes*. She invests these, often colourless rôles, with great authority and feeling, and with a dignity and beauty of movement that recalls the days when she was one of the ballerinas of the Company.

She joined the Sadler's Wells School in 1933, and soon afterwards was in the *corps de ballet* of the Company. Her first rôle was in 1934 in the *pas de trois* in *Le Lac des Cygnes* and from this time her progress though slow was assured.

She showed herself to be a sensitive artist, in tune perfectly with the mood and feeling of every ballet in which she appeared. Her technique grew in strength, and in the classical ballets, in particular, she had a magnificent line and control. She could express a wide range of emotion, from the tragic weakness of the Red Queen in *Checkmate*, to the doting and ridiculous mother in *Bonne Bouche*.

Her list of outstanding rôles is long, but among those which must be mentioned are Swanilda, Princess Aurora, the Lilac Fairy and in the Bluebird *pas de deux* in *The Sleeping Princess*, the Swan Queen in *Le Lac des Cygnes*, Queen of the Wilis in *Giselle*, the Moon in *Horoscope*, a Child of Light in *Dante Sonata* and in *Les Sylphides* and *Symphonic Variations*.

de Marney

IN BONNE BOUCHE

SWANILDA   *Anthony*

IN DANTE SONATA   *Baron*

PRINCESS AURORA   *Baron*

IN LES SYLPHIDES   *Anthony*

Anthony

THE LILAC FAIRY IN THE SLEEPING BEAUTY

BERYL GREY

Beryl Grey entered the Sadler's Wells School at the age of nine, and in 1941, when she was barely fourteen, she became a member of the *corps de ballet*. Ninette de Valois had not been slow to recognise her astonishing talent while she was still at school, and soon after she joined the Company she was dancing solo parts. It is true that the first opportunity to dance a solo was due to the indisposition of one of the soloists, but before long she had added to the rôle of The Lady in Helpmann's *Comus*, the Polka in *Façade*, and Prayer in *Coppélia*. She danced the *pas de deux* in *Les Sylphides* and the Lilac Fairy in *The Sleeping Princess* before she was fifteen, and on her fifteenth birthday she danced Odette-Odile in *Le Lac des Cygnes* at the New Theatre, London.

She has progressed greatly as a dancer and as an artist since that first astonishing performance of Odette-Odile, but even at that time she showed those qualities that have always distinguished her work : " The sheer joy of movement," as Arnold Haskell has so rightly described it, a musicality that makes her dancing flow with the music, a lyric warmth and beauty, and a serenity and ease in dancing that allows no sign of strain however demanding is the rôle.

To these qualities must be added her dramatic sense, first displayed most notably as the Duessa in Ashton's *The Quest*, in the Black Queen of *Checkmate*, and as Death in *Donald of the Burthens*.

She is tall, five feet six and a half inches, which might have been a dis-advantage to a less gifted dancer since every fault is magnified. But with Beryl Grey, her height adds to her authority, and she uses her long arms with a fluent grace and dramatic force.

One lovely quality she possesses, is a radiance that makes her performances in the classical ballets a special joy. Her Giselle, her Odette-Odile and her Aurora may never reach the heights of Fonteyn's, but they are completely satisfying. And whether the part she is dancing is the principal rôle, or a subsidiary one such as the Lilac Fairy in *The Sleeping Beauty*, Winter in *Cinderella*, or the second dancer in *Ballet Imperial*, makes no difference to the zest and attack she brings to her dancing. She has the true ballerina quality of lifting the performance whenever she appears. Her magnificent physique sustains her through even the most arduous rôle and always she appears to have something in reserve.

ODETTE IN LE LAC DES CYGNES

19

MOIRA SHEARER

J. T. Knight

WITH DAVID PALTENGHI IN LES PATINEURS

Moria Shearer was a pupil of the Sadler's Wells School in the early months of the war, but her training at the School was interrupted when her parents sent her for safety to Scotland, and she made her first appearance on the stage as a soloist with International Ballet in 1941. In 1942 she returned to Sadler's Wells as a student, first appearing with the Company towards the end of the year. It was not long before she was dancing as a soloist in *Les Sylphides*, and this was followed by a succession of other rôles, including Columbine in *Le Carnaval*, and the Young Girl in *Le Spectre de la Rose*.

Her first ballerina rôle was Aurora in *The Sleeping Beauty* in 1946, soon after the Sadler's Wells Ballet had moved to Covent Garden. Of this first performance Arnold Haskell wrote (in *The Ballet Annual* No. 1) " Shearer has an attack and a self-possession altogether unusual in a young British dancer, gaining the sympathy and then the enthusiasm of the audience from the moment that she steps on to the stage. Never was a dancer less apologetic for any errors of technique, with the result that technical shortcomings due to inexperience are not noticed. Shearer has a magnificently fluid style, great and unusual beauty and a fine intelligence. In a year's time, when her technique has caught up with her very conscious artistry, she should become an outstanding member of the company. She is in the potential ballerina class."

In 1946, she also danced for the first time Swanilda and Odette-Odile, and with Margot Fonteyn and Pamela May she appeared in Ashton's *Symphonic Variations*, her auburn beauty contrasting admirably with the fair beauty of Pamela May and the dark beauty of Fonteyn. Giselle she danced for the first time in 1948, and later she created the rôle of Cinderella, owing to Fonteyn's absence through illness.

By this time she had already become a film star—appearing with great success as a dancer in *The Red Shoes*. Since then ballet has seen less of her, and she is no longer a member of the Sadler's Wells Ballet, although she has appeared as a guest artist. More recently she has danced with Festival Ballet, speaking with success the lines recited in *Alice in Wonderland*, and a later venture was her appearance as Titania in *A Midsummer Night's Dream*, in which she made her first appearance as an actress who dances, rather than as a dancer who acts. Whatever her success as an actress, and in films it is already assured, ballet-goers will always have many happy memories of the time when she was a ballerina of Sadler's Wells.

PRINCESS AURORA IN THE SLEEPING BEAUTY

Houston Rogers

CINDERELLA

VIOLETTA ELVIN

Violetta Elvin first appeared with the Sadler's Wells Ballet as a guest artist on 21st February 1946, the second night of the Company's first season at the Royal Opera House, Covent Garden, dancing in the Bluebird *pas de deux*.

She danced in the Bluebird with an attack and charm that aroused great enthusiasm. She soon became a permanent member of the Company and her exceptional talents were soon seen in other ballets in the repertoire. She danced in *Les Sylphides*, *Les Patineurs*, *Les Sirènes*, *Balabille*, *Le Carnaval* (Columbine), *Checkmate*, *Le Tricorne* (The Miller's Wife) and in other ballets.

Her first appearance in the ballerina rôles aroused great interest. She was at that time the only leading dancer who had not been trained in the Sadler's Wells organisation. Of Russian parentage, she had received her training at the Bolshoi Ballet School in Moscow. She had been a soloist with the Bolshoi Company, and at the age of eighteen she had danced Odette-Odile at the Tashkent State Theatre.

Violetta Elvin has great authority on the stage, and she dances with the vigour and attack in which Russian dancers excel. She has a noble carriage, a strong line seen at its best in her superb arabesques, and she makes exquisite use of her arms. She conveys the charm and emotion of a rôle through her dancing, relying less on facial expression than some dancers, and her Giselle and her Odette particularly are most moving.

Miss Elvin has danced in most of the modern repertoire of the Company and she is outstanding in *Ballet Imperial*, in a rôle which suits her special style to perfection, in *Veneziana*, as Queen of the Waters in Ashton's *Homage to the Queen*, as Sylvia, and as Cinderella.

At her best Miss Elvin is superb. With magnificent authority, a strong controlled technique and with charm and radiance, she carries all before her.

Above : Queen of the Waters in *Homage to the Queen*   *Houston Rogers*

Left : With Giulio Perugini in *Le Lac des Cygnes* at La Scala, Milan, where she appeared as a guest artist with great success.

Piccagliani, Milan

Below : Odette in *Le Lac des Cygnes* at Covent Garden.

An action photograph by Helga Sharland

NADIA NERINA

Felix Fonteyn

AS SYLVIA WITH ALEXIS RASSINE

Anthony

IN LES SYLPHIDES

Nadia Nerina came from South Africa to England towards the end of 1945, and in February 1946 she joined the Sadler's Wells Ballet School. The following year she became a member of the Sadler's Wells Theatre Ballet, dancing at first under the name of Nadia Moore. Her vitality and the strength of her technique, made her outstanding in a company of most promising young dancers, and she was, in one critic's view, reminiscent of Baronova, one of the brilliant young ballerinas of de Basil's Ballets Russe.

Nadia Nerina appeared in several of the new ballets produced by the Company in 1946–47 : as the Circus Dancer in *Mardi Gras*, as Khadra in the ballet of that name, and in a strong dramatic part in Anthony Burke's *The Vagabonds* she was outstanding. She joined the senior company on December 1st, 1947, and two days later she danced her first solo rôle, the Mazurka in *Les Sylphides*.

She was soon dancing other soloist rôles, and in 1948 Ashton created for her in *Cinderella*, the rôle of Fairy Spring, which suited perfectly her joyful ebullience. She always dances as though she enjoys dancing and she conveys her joy to the audience.

Early in 1951, on the first night of Ashton's *Daphnis and Chloé*, she appeared as Odette in Act II of *Le Lac des Cygnes*. It was a good performance technically and held out great promise for the future. This promise is now being fulfilled, and in the full-length version of the ballet, she shows a personal interpretation which is progressing steadily. And so it is with all her work : as the Princess Aurora, as Cinderella, and as Sylvia, she is gaining new confidence and poise and, what is more important, more character and feeling. One of her outstanding performances at present is Swanilda in *Coppélia*. She surmounts the considerable technical difficulties of the rôle with ease and makes Swanilda what she should be, a gay, and mischievous peasant girl.

IN A WEDDING BOUQUET

Roger Wood

CINDERELLA

The absence of Margot Fonteyn, Beryl Grey and Violetta Elvin at various times in 1953 and 1954 gave her exceptional opportunities to dance the major rôles in the Sadler's Wells repertoire, and Miss Elvin's retirement from the American tour of 1953–54, owing to a serious accident, brought Miss Nerina into new prominence. She was a great success in America and John Martin, the distinguished critic of the *New York Times*, found her "completely adorable."

" She is pretty as a picture," he continued in his review of her Princess Aurora, " has great charm and can dance like a million dollars. Her body is beautifully placed, giving her lovely, free arms and an unusually articulated torso.

IN HOMAGE TO THE QUEEN

Houston Rogers

There are simply no problems of movement for her, and never so much as a hint of an ugly one. When Miss Nerina has developed a musical phrase to equal her command of the physical medium, we shall all be fighting to drink champagne out of her slippers."

In the modern repertoire she is especially delightful as Mam'zelle Angot, and in a rôle which is poles apart from Angot's gay frivolity, the ballerina rôle in Ashton's *Scènes de Ballets*, she brings great beauty of line and expression.

Nadia Nerina has verve and style, she has great confidence and a crisp and assured technique. She has charm, good looks, great vitality and a natural gaiety. But above all, it is by her hard work and intelligence that she has become in a few years a dancer of the ballerina class. She is now only at the beginning of her career as a ballerina, and the years that lie ahead should be for her years of steady progress and fulfilment.

ROWENA JACKSON

In recent years an increasing number of dancers in the Company has been recruited from the Dominions, and outstanding among them are Nadia Nerina from South Africa and Rowena Jackson from New Zealand. In 1941 Miss Jackson won the first Royal Academy of Dancing scholarship to be awarded to a dancer in the Dominions. The war prevented her coming to England to take up the scholarship, and it was not until 1946 that she was able to come to this country, when she joined the Sadler's Wells School. In 1947 she was awarded the Adeline Genée Gold Medal and later the same year she joined the Sadler's Wells Ballet at Covent Garden.

Of her technical brilliance there was no doubt, and her

Baron

WITH MICHAEL SOMES IN LE LAC DES CYGNES

IN SCENES DE BALLET

Allen

first successes were in ballets which demanded technique rather than character in interpretation. It was in *Les Patineurs*, the most popular of all Ashton's one-act ballets at Covent Garden, that she first attracted attention. As one of the girls in blue, in the part created originally by Mary Honer, she astonished the audience by the brilliance of her *fouettés en tournant*, and rumour had it that she could do 150 *fouettés* without a break, just for the fun of it. She added to her reputation for technical fireworks in *Scènes de Ballet* and *Ballet Imperial*.

Rowena Jackson had from the outset a distinctive appearance on the stage, a glamour and a sparkle that at once attracted attention, and she was, it seemed, a reliable and confident dancer. Then, early in 1953, she danced Odette-Odile in *Le Lac des Cygnes*.

It was a performance of considerable promise, which is high praise indeed. No dancer of her experience could be expected to give a full-blooded interpretation of this arduous and difficult rôle. Individual interpretation, and no other interpretation is valid, must develop through the years.

The American critics, who had not seen her as a principal dancer until the tour of 1953–54, praised her performances highly. " Miss Jackson is crisp, sharp, accurate, with a sense of reserve force beyond even the brilliance she gives us," wrote John Martin in the *New York Times*, and in another review he wrote : " Young Rowena Jackson . . . is definitely on the way up. Technically, she is breathtaking, and her turns are the fastest things (as well as the straightest and cleanest) you are likely to see anywhere."

As Miss Jackson learns to feel from within, rather than imposing a character from without, so will her interpretations of the ballerina rôles improve and develop, and give her a wider variety of emotional expression.

Already her dancing is losing the angularity it once had and a brittle quality that showed a lack of musical sensitivity, and she is gaining a new warmth and softness that are good signs for her future development.

28

ROWENA JACKSON WITH BRYAN ASHBRIDGE IN LE LAC DES CYGNES

Houston Rogers

Duncan Melvin

IN THE OPERA " ORPHEUS "

A photograph which shows the charm and grace of this young dancer

SVETLANA BERIOSOVA

Svetlana Beriosova made her début with the Sadler's Wells Ballet at the Royal Opera House, Covent Garden, on 3rd July 1952, as the Lilac Fairy in *The Sleeping Beauty*. It was an admirable rôle for her introduction to Covent Garden, and one well suited to the special qualities which distinguish her as a dancer. But it was, none the less, an exacting task for any dancer to assume for the first time, an important part in a full-length ballet, and on the enormous stage of Covent Garden. But she showed few signs of the ordeal : she had great confidence and authority, a gracious elegance and charm, and if the inner glow which the Lilac Fairy should radiate was only a little light, there was every sign that with time she would become outstanding in the part.

Svetlana is the daughter of a dancer, Nicholas Beriosoff, now *régisseur* of Festival Ballet, and from the time of her birth in 1932 in Lithuania, where her father was a member of the State Ballet,

all her life has been spent in the world of ballet. While still of school age she was in the *corps de ballet* of the Marquis de Cuevas's Company, of which her father was *maître de ballet*, and when he later held a similar position with Metropolitan Ballet, she joined the Company, and danced soloist parts. On her appearance in London with the Company, she at once attracted the critics' attention in Frank Staff's *Fanciulla delle Rose*, and Taras's *Designs for Strings*, and a little later, for a most moving interpretation of Odette, in *Le Lac des Cygnes*, Act II. Metropolitan Ballet had a short life, and Miss Beriosova

Paul Wilson

REHEARSING FOR A TELEVISION PERFORMANCE OF LES SYLPHIDES, WITH MARKOVA AND KARSAVINA

WITH MICHAEL SOMES IN RINALDO AND ARMIDA

then joined the Sadler's Wells Theatre Ballet. Among a company of young dancers of her own age, she seemed to be astonishingly mature, and not altogether at home. Her style of dancing, noticeably different from the rest of the Company, was seen to its best advantage in *Casse-Noisette* and in *Coppélia*. Her Swanilda was hailed as one of the finest for many years.

After her début at Covent Garden she appeared in many other ballets in the repertoire, creating her first important part in 1953, in Cranko's new ballet *The Shadow*.

She is essentially a classical dancer, and a dancer, one feels instinctively, of the ballerina class, with her noble carriage, the finish and perfection of her dancing, her musicality, her authority and command of the stage, and, what has been so rightly called, her elusive air of nobility.

The season at Covent Garden in 1954 after the Company's return from America, was for her, in particular, a time of opportunity and achievement. She danced Swanilda at the second performance of the splendid new production of *Coppélia* on 4th March, and a few days later at a Royal Gala, on 9th March, she was Queen of the Waters in Ashton's *Homage to the Queen*, her fellow queens being Fonteyn, Nerina and Jackson. On 14th April she danced the title-rôle in Ashton's full-length ballet, *Sylvia*, and on the 1st June the Princess Aurora in *The Sleeping Beauty*. It was a magnificent and exciting first performance. She seemed to have been born to dance Aurora.

In the splendid revival of *The Firebird* in 1954 Beriosova was the Princess. She made her a gentle lady, youthful but dignified, noble and gracious, and a splendid foil to the virile Prince of Michael Somes.

In January 1955, in Ashton's short ballet drama, *Rinaldo and Armida* which was virtually a long *pas de deux* for Somes and Beriosova, she won fresh laurels for her performance as the enchanted Armida. In February 1955 she danced, for the first time in this country, Odette-Odile. Her dancing at this performance had uneasy moments, due perhaps to first night nerves, but later performances showed a remarkable improvement.

Beriosova's official promotion to ballerina came in 1955, shortly before the Company left for its American tour.

She has so many gifts, which training and technique cannot provide, and at the beginning of her career as a ballerina, with a great future before her, one can only wish for two more blessings to be bestowed upon her : stamina and staying power, and the gift of humanity, which Karsavina and Fonteyn and all great artists possess, to their immeasurable benefit, and ours.

Maurice Seymour

SVETLANA BERIOSOVA
AS ODETTE IN LE LAC DES CYGNES